GRIFFINS AND PHOENIXES

Cavendish
Square

New York

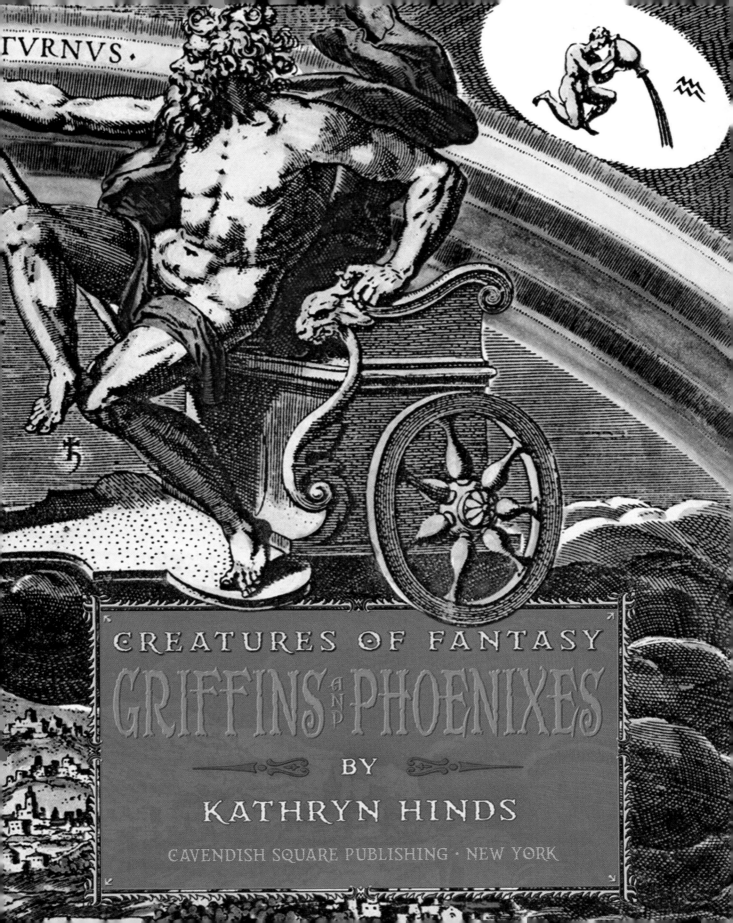

CREATURES OF FANTASY
GRIFFINS and PHOENIXES

BY
KATHRYN HINDS

CAVENDISH SQUARE PUBLISHING · NEW YORK

To Sorscha

Published in 2014 by Cavendish Square Publishing, LLC
303 Park Avenue South, Suite 1247, New York, NY 10010

Copyright © 2014 by Cavendish Square Publishing, LLC

First Edition

Website: cavendishsq.com

This publication represents the opinions and views of the author based on his or her personal experience, knowledge, and research. The information in this book serves as a general guide only. The author and publisher have used their best efforts in preparing this book and disclaim liability rising directly or indirectly from the use and application of this book.

CPSIA Compliance Information: Batch #WS13CSQ

All websites were available and accurate when this book was sent to press.

LIBRARY OF CONGRESS CATALOGING-IN-PUBLICATION DATA

Hinds, Kathryn, 1962- Griffins and phoenixes / Kathryn Hinds. p. cm.—(Creatures of fantasy) Includes bibliographical references and index. Summary: "Explores the mythical and historical backgrounds of griffins and phoenixes, including the hippogriff, monster birds of the Middle East (rukh, Simorgh, anqa), the giant condor, and the Thunder Birds of the Americas"—Provided by publisher. ISBN 978-0-7614-4923-2 (hardcover)—ISBN 978-1-62712-052-4 (paperback)—ISBN 978-1-60870-681-5 (ebook) 1. Griffins. 2. Phoenix (Mythical bird) 3. Animals, Mythical. I. Title. BL325.G7H56 2013 398'.469—dc23 2012000518

Editor: Deborah Grahame-Smith   Art Director: Anahid Hamparian   Series Designer: Michael Nelson

Photo research by Debbie Needleman. The photographs in this book are used by permission and through the courtesy of: Front Cover: © ZUMA Press/Newscom. Back cover: © dbimages/Alamy. Page i: © ullstein bild – histopics/The Image Works; pages ii-iii: akg-images/Newscom; page vi: Image copyright © The Metropolitan Museum of Art. Image source: Art Resource, NY; page 8: © Rui Saraiva/Alamy; page 10: © Mary Evans Picture Library/Alamy; page 11: © DEA/G. DAGLI ORTI/Getty Images; page 12: © Robert Morris/Alamy; pages 14, 35, 36: © akg-images/Newscom; page 16: Koninklijke Bibliotheek - National Library of the Netherlands, from The Liber Floridus of Lambert of St. Omer. KB, 72A 23, Folio 46r; page 18: © Eileen Tweedy/The Art Archive at Art Resource, NY; page 19: © Lebrecht 3/Lebrecht Music & Arts/Corbis; page 20: © The Art Gallery Collection/Alamy; page 21: Ms 651/1486 Alexander III the Great returning to the ground in his flying machine, from the "Roman d'Alexandré" (vellum) (detail of 210366). German School (15th century)/Musee Conde, Chantilly, France/Giraudon/The Bridgeman Art Library; page 22: The Mighty Roc. Escott, Dan (1928 – 1987)/Private Collection/© Look and Learn/The Bridgeman Art Library; page 24: Sinbad the Sailor. Quinto, Nadir (1918 – 1994). Private Collection/© Look and Learn/The Bridgeman Art Library; page 27: © Universal Images Group/Art Resource, NY; page 30: © Caren Loebel-Fried/Getty Images; page 32: © akg-images/James Morris/Newscom; page 37: © The Trustees of the British Museum/Art Resource, NY; page 38: © Mary Evans Picture Library/Alamy; page 40: © John Henshall/Alamy; page 42: Yoshitsune and the Tengu-King (color woodblock print). Yoshitoshi, Tsukioka (1839 – 1892). Private Collection/The Bridgeman Art Library; page 43: © Nigel Norrington/ArenaPal/The Image Works; page 44: © Tom McHugh/Photo Researchers, Inc.; page 47: © Lebrecht Music and Arts Photo Library/Alamy; page 48: © Robert Fried/Alamy; page 50: © Werner Forman Archive/Museum of the American Indian, Heye Foundation, New York, USA/Glow Images; page 54: © bpk, Berlin/Ethnologisches Museum, Staatliche Museen, Berlin, Germany/ Photo by Gisela Oestreich /Art Resource, NY; page 55: © Werner Forman Archive/Provincial Museum, Victoria, British Columbia/Glow Images.

Printed in the United States of America

front cover: Griffins like this one carry adventurers from place to place in the computer game World of Warcraft.
half-title: This 1493 illustration had a Latin caption that translates, "Phoenix, the one-of-a-kind bird."
title page: An image from the late 1550s shows the ancient Roman god Saturn riding in a chariot pulled by two snake-tailed griffins.
back cover: One of the many phoenixes that decorate the Hall of Prayer for Good Harvest in the Temple of Heaven in Beijing, China.

CONTENTS

A twelve-inch-high bronze griffin, made around 1400 in Germany.

INTRODUCTION

In the CREATURES OF FANTASY series we celebrate the deeds of dragons, unicorns, and their kin. These fabulous beasts have inhabited the imagination and arts since the beginnings of human history, immortalized in paintings and sculptures, mythology and literature, movies and video games. Today's blockbuster fantasy novels and films—*The Chronicles of Narnia, Harry Potter, Lord of the Rings, Eragon,* and others—have brought new popularity to the denizens of folklore, myth, and legend. It seems that these creatures of the imagination have always been with us and, in one way or another, always will be.

Belief in the fantastic, in wonders, appears to be a lasting part of the human experience. Even if we no longer believe that dragons and unicorns actually exist, we still like to think about what the world might be like if they did. We dream and daydream about them. We make up stories. And as we share those dreams, read and tell those stories, we not only stir our imaginations, but also explore some of the deepest hopes and fears of humanity. The power of the dragon, the purity of the unicorn, the mystery of the sphinx, the allure of the mermaid—these and more are all part of our human heritage, the legends of our ancestors still alive for us today.

GRIFFINS: ANCIENT GUARDIANS

I hear that the griffin is a quadruped like a lion,
with talons of enormous strength. . . .
It is reputed to have black plumage on its back
with a red chest and white wings.
~Aelian, *On Animals*, 3rd century

ITS NAME HAS BEEN SPELLED *GRIFFIN, GRIFFON, gryphon*, and a number of other ways. It has been given a variety of features: a falcon's head, an eagle's head; a lion's tail, a snake's tail; a delicate curving beak, a sharp hooked beak; pointed ears, floppy ears, no ears. Ram horns, a crown, a topknot, or a peacock's crest might ornament its head. It nearly always has wings—but occasionally it doesn't. Sometimes it resembles a dragon so closely that the only way to tell the difference is to remember that dragons have scales, while griffins have fur and feathers. So what makes a griffin a griffin? In general, its back half is mainly a lion, and its front half is mainly a bird of prey. A combination of the fiercest and most regal animals of land and sky, the griffin is a proud, powerful, and ancient creature.

Opposite: This fierce creature, which has watched over Fleet Street in London since 1880, is said by some to be a griffin and by others to be a dragon.

The Gryphon was among many strange creatures Alice met in Wonderland. Here, the Gryphon and the Mock Turtle show Alice how to do a dance called the Lobster Quadrille.

ELOQUENT IMAGES

In *Alice's Adventures in Wonderland* (1865), author Lewis Carroll told his readers, "If you don't know what a Gryphon is, look at the picture." Indeed, we first meet the griffin in artwork. Long before anyone wrote down anything about this beast, people were making paintings and sculptures of it. The oldest known image of a griffin was crafted in Persia (modern Iran) about five thousand years ago. Not long afterward, griffins began to show up in Egyptian art.

Ancient Egyptian griffins were lion bodied with wings and had the heads of hawks or falcons—birds that represented the sun. As time went on, artists added a royal crown to the bird's head. The Egyptian griffin, symbol of both the sun's daily victory over darkness and the king's victories over hostile forces, was often shown trampling a serpent or a group of Egypt's enemies. An ancient Egyptian writer proclaimed the griffin to be earth's mightiest creature, "with the beak of a falcon, the eyes of a man, the body of a lion, the ears of a fish, the tail of a snake." Eventually, though, Egyptians replaced the griffin with another emblem of royal and solar strength, the sphinx—a lion with a human head.*

Between the realms of Egypt and Persia lay Mesopotamia, today's Iraq. This fertile land was home to a number of ancient civilizations, many of which portrayed griffins in their art. The Mesopotamian griffin could be a terrifying creature allied with

*For more on the sphinx and other part-human creatures, see *Sphinxes and Centaurs*, another volume in the CREATURES OF FANTASY series.

demons or with underworld deities. Other deities, however, might tame and control these formidable beasts, to pull their chariots or guard their thrones. Many images show a goddess or god standing between two guardian griffins, often gripping each beast by the paw or neck in a show of mastery.

Griffin imagery spread around the Middle East and beyond. Two of the most elegant griffins in ancient art graced the walls of a throne room in Knossos, Crete, an island in the Mediterranean Sea. Sir Arthur Evans, the archaeologist who explored the palace ruins in the early 1900s, described the crouching griffins "guarding in one case a vision of the Goddess herself and her divine associates on the altar ledge beyond, in the other the seat of honour of her terrestrial [earthly] viceregent, the Priest-king." The people of Crete and elsewhere also put images of griffins on coffins and tombs, probably to protect the dead person's spirit on its journey into the afterlife.

This griffin guarded a wall in the palace of Darius I, who ruled Persia from 522 to 486 BCE.

GRIFFINS AND GOLD

Everyone in the ancient world seemed to agree that griffins were formidable guardians. Greek art began to show griffins around 1400 BCE, often portraying them as protectors of the rising sun. They were companions of Dionysos, god of grape vines and other growing things, and of the god of light, Apollo, who was often shown riding a griffin or driving a griffin-drawn chariot. Apollo's sister, the moon goddess Artemis, was also sometimes depicted on a griffin's back. Later, griffins became associated with Nemesis, a goddess of justice who pursued evildoers as swiftly and fiercely as the griffins that pulled her chariot.

The Greeks knew griffins as guardians not only of justice, growing things, and the golden sun, but also of golden treasure. Around 430 BCE, the Greek historian Herodotus wrote about gold that came from a place far to the east and north: "I cannot say for sure how the gold is obtained there, but some say that one-eyed men called Arimaspeans steal it from griffins." Some of Herodotus's griffin information came from Aristeas, a traveler who had lived two hundred years earlier. Aristeas had written a poem (now lost) about his search for the fabled land beyond the home of the North Wind, where Apollo was said to spend the winters. While journeying through central Asia, Aristeas learned of the Arimaspians and their conflict with the gold-guarding griffins.

Herodotus is known as the Father of History because of his research and writings on the Persians and other peoples of western Asia.

The same story was referred to in *Prometheus Bound*, a tragedy by the playwright Aeschylus (d. 456 BCE). Prometheus was the ancient being who stole fire from the gods to give to humanity. Zeus, the king of the gods, condemned Prometheus to be chained to mountains far in the east, at the very edge of the world known to the Greeks. In the play, Prometheus warns another character, "Beware the sharp-beaked hounds of Zeus that bark not, the griffins, and the one-eyed Arimaspian folk, mounted on horses, who dwell about the . . . stream that flows with gold."

Around 400 BCE a Greek doctor named Ctesias, who spent many years at the Persian royal court, wrote that there were griffins in India (which, to the ancient Greeks, included Tibet and surrounding regions): "Gold also is a product of India. It is . . . found on those many high-towering mountains which are inhabited by the Griffons, a race of four-footed birds, about as large as wolves, having legs and claws like those of the lion. . . . On account of those birds the gold with which the mountains abound is difficult to be got."

In fact, the mountains that edged the plains of central Asia were the sources of much of the gold that eventually made its way to ancient Persia, Greece, and Mesopotamia. The gold was mined, worked, and traded by nomadic peoples generally called Scythians (who lived on the western plains) and Sakas (farther east). These peoples loved artwork, including golden ornaments, featuring fantastic creatures of all kinds—but griffins were among the favorites. Important Sakas, both women and men, were even tattooed with images of griffins.

The Sakas and Scythians may have had real-life models for their griffin artwork. In many of the very places where gold was mined, strange skeletons could be found under the soil or even on the surface, laid bare by erosion. Six to eight feet long, they had four limbs, long tails, and large-beaked, crested skulls. Although there was no indication of wings, the skeletons had a rather birdlike look about them—and they were sometimes found near nests full of eggs. Scientists now know that these fossils belonged to a dinosaur, *Protoceratops*. But to people who didn't know about dinosaurs, the best way to explain the skeletons of four-legged beaked creatures discovered near gold deposits was to call them the remains of gold-guarding griffins.

LATER GRIFFINS AND GRIFFIN KIN

The griffon is bigger and stronger than eight lions . . .
and bigger and stronger than a hundred eagles.
For certainly he will carry to his nest in flight a great horse
with a man on his back, or two oxen yoked together,
as they work together at the plough.
~Sir John Mandeville, *Travels,* 1371

GRIFFIN LORE GREW AND SPREAD OVER TIME. The first-century Roman geographer Pomponius Mela wrote about a far-northern country that was uninhabitable "because the Griffons (a cruel and eager kind of wild beast) do wonderfully love the gold, which lies discovered above the ground . . . and are very fierce upon them that touch it." Another first-century Roman, Pliny the Elder, summarized the common knowledge about griffins and their archenemies, the one-eyed Arimaspians: "These people wage continual war around their mines with the griffins, a kind of wild beast with wings . . . that digs gold out of mines, which the creatures guard and the Arimaspi try to take from them, both with remarkable covetousness [greed]."

Opposite: This griffin from a German children's book published in 1792 looks alert but much friendlier than the fierce, greedy creatures described by ancient authors.

A popular encyclopedia from the Middle Ages began its chapter on winged creatures with a description and illustration of the griffin's cruelty.

Pliny's account had great influence over the following centuries, as did the work of Gaius Julius Solinus, written around 200. Solinus described griffins as "cruel beyond all the bounds of fury." He also said that griffins would tear a person to pieces on sight. It seemed to him that they must have been created specifically to punish people who were too eager to obtain gold. Such writings led to the griffin becoming a symbol of greed and sin during the Middle Ages (roughly 500 to 1500).

The Symbolic Griffin

Some of the most popular books during the Middle Ages were bestiaries, collections of stories about both real and imaginary animals—although all of the animals were real to readers of the time. Here is how one bestiary described the griffin: "It is fearsome to see for it has the body and claws of the lion and the wings, head, and fierce beak of the eagle. All men should fear it because it feasts upon them at any opportunity. It is also extremely fond of eating horses. It is seen in these parts but rarely as it lives mostly in high mountains or in Hyperborean [far northern] lands."

One writer claimed that the griffin's northern homeland symbolized its distance from the light of kindness and charity, and so the griffin itself represented "the cruel criminality of the powerful who ferociously drink up human deaths." By 1200 people were often comparing greedy nobles to griffins. The English scholar Alexander Neckam, however, thought this comparison was unfair to the griffins: "Griffins dig up gold and gloat over its shining brilliance; their eyes delight in the yellow metal. If you think they are like the nobles, you are wrong: the nobles are spurred on by their greedy hunger for gold, whilst the griffins have no nagging desire for lucre [profit] but naturally rejoice in the quiet pursuit of looking."

Most religious writers did not agree with Neckam's opinion on the griffins' lack of greed. In fact, it had become a common belief that griffins liked to hoard not only gold but also precious gems, especially emeralds—and griffins apparently fought the Arimaspians even harder for emeralds than they did for gold. Since the emerald was a symbol for Christian faith, a twelfth-century writer explained, the griffins represented "the devils who envy men the precious jewel of faith and who want to possess it." He added that the one-eyed Arimaspians represented all those who, single-mindedly devoted to God, "defend the grace of faith which the griffins—that is, the devils—want to take away from them."

At the same time, though, some authors used the griffin as a symbol of Jesus. Its lion body was said to represent his earthly nature as a man, while its eagle wings and head stood for his heavenly nature as the Son of God. Other writers stopped short of identifying the griffin with Jesus, but focused on the creature's strength and powers of protection. Sculptures and other images of griffins guarded many churches, doorways, and tombs. Artists sometimes showed a griffin standing watch over the tree of life in the Garden of Eden, warning sinners to beware of temptation.

A number of cities, organizations, and families adopted the griffin as their own personal symbol of protection. Knights and nobles were especially drawn to the strength, bravery, pride, and ferocity of the griffin and featured it on their shields and coats of arms. Such

The griffin-adorned shield of one of the noble families of fifteenth-century Florence, Italy.

uses remained popular even after people stopped believing in the existence of griffins. As the English author Thomas Browne wrote in 1646, the griffin was not a real animal but was still a powerful symbol: "an Emblem of valour and magnanimity, as being compounded of the Eagle and the Lion, the noblest animals in their kinds."

The Griffin's Improbable Child

Because the Arimaspians rode on horses when they went to steal gold from the griffins, people long believed that griffins and horses were mortal enemies. The Roman poet Virgil once used the expression "Griffins must be mating with horses" to refer to a situation that seemed crazily impossible, or perhaps miraculous. When the Italian poet Ludovico Ariosto created a beast that was the offspring of a griffin and a mare, he was making a kind of literary joke inspired by Virgil. Ariosto called his winged creation a hippogriff.

In Ariosto's 1532 epic poem *Orlando Furioso*, the hippogriff was introduced as the steed of a great magician:

But yet the beast he rode was not of art
But gotten of a griffin and a mare
And like a griffin had the former part,
And wings and head and claws that hideous are
And passing strength and force and [daring] heart,
But all the rest may with a horse compare. . . .
This monster rare from farthest regions brought
This rare magician ordered with such skill
That in one month or little more he taught
The savage monster to obey his will.

The magician gave the hippogriff to a famous knight, and the two flew around the world doing brave deeds. Eventually the hippogriff carried another worthy knight to paradise and beyond, all the way to the moon. Hippogriffs have continued to fascinate writers and readers, as well as artists and filmmakers, with the result that Ariosto's old literary joke has become a full-fledged fantastic creature.

Artist Gustave Doré featured the hippogriff on his cover for an 1877 edition of *Orlando Furioso*.

More Four-Footed Flyers

Griffins and hippogriffs were not the only flying quadrupeds (animals with four feet) to populate literature, legends, and art. A winged lion was the symbol of the Italian city of Venice, which controlled a powerful empire for more than four centuries. Venice adopted the winged lion because it was the emblem of the city's patron saint, or holy protector, Saint Mark. This imagery was based on a Bible passage in which the prophet Ezekiel had a vision of four winged creatures, each with the face of a man, an eagle, an ox, and a lion. In the early Middle Ages, people interpreted Ezekiel's vision as a reference to the four authors of the Gospels, the Bible books that tell the life story of Jesus. Saint Mark wasn't the only Gospel author to be pictured as a winged quadruped—Saint Luke was often portrayed as a winged ox.

Winged lions and bulls had also featured in the artwork of ancient Persia and Mesopotamia. So had winged deer and antelope. The Scythians and Sakas depicted all kinds of animals with wings, including tigers and snow leopards. Winged tigers appeared in the art of ancient China, too. An ivory ornament from the ancient African kingdom of Kush portrayed a winged giraffe. And

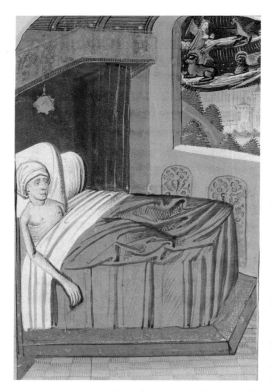

This is how a fifteenth-century artist imagined the prophet Ezekiel having his vision of the four winged creatures.

the mythology of India tells of Airavata, a white elephant with beautiful wings. Created at the beginning of time, Airavata became the mount of the sky and war god Indra. As Airavata flew through the air, he used his trunk to suck up water from under the earth and to spray it down as life-giving rain.

One of Greek mythology's most famous flying quadrupeds was Pegasus. This handsome winged horse had a rather gruesome beginning. When his mother, the snake-haired monster Medusa, was beheaded, Pegasus was born from her blood. He immediately leaped into the air, spread his wings, and soared through the sky. Flying was as natural to him as running was to other horses.

Pegasus became the steed of the young hero Bellerophon, carrying him from one adventure to another. The pair's most difficult task was to destroy the Chimera, a terrible fire-breathing monster that was part lion, part goat, and part snake. After they succeeded in killing the Chimera, Bellerophon was so proud that he directed Pegasus to carry him to the heavenly dwelling of the great gods. But Zeus, king of the deities, sent a fly to sting Pegasus so that he bucked and threw Bellerophon from his back. Then, according to the early Greek poet Hesiod, Pegasus "came to the immortals, and there he lives in the household of Zeus, and carries the thunder and lightning for Zeus of the counsels."

ALEXANDER AND THE GRIFFINS

Alexander the Great lived in the 300s BCE and had a spectacular career as a conqueror, winning an empire that included Greece, Egypt, and Persia. During the Middle Ages he became an extremely popular hero, whose story was told in a book called *The Romance of Alexander*. This book had many versions in many languages, but all featured numerous fantastical adventures. In one episode, Alexander had reached the mountains of India, said to be the ends of the earth. Some versions of the tale say that he wanted to see if this was really true; other versions say he decided that since he had conquered all the earth, he would try to conquer the sky as well. Either way, he had a plan:

> When he came down the mountain, he ordered his master workers to build a chair with iron bars on each side. And four Gryphons were tied to the chair with iron chains, and over the chair he put meat, just far enough from the Gryphons that they flew upward and carried Alexander into the air. The earth seemed so small, and the sea looked like a dragon encircling the earth. Then, suddenly, God's mysterious veil enveloped the Gryphons and forced them to land in a field, a ten day march from the army, but Alexander was not hurt.

In another version, the flight ended when, as Alexander himself narrated, "A flying creature in the form of a man approached me and said, 'O Alexander, you have not yet secured the whole earth, and are you now exploring the heavens? Return to earth as fast as possible, or you will become food for those birds.' . . . Thus admonished by Providence above, I returned to earth."

Above: Returning to earth, Alexander releases the griffins who carried him aloft.

MONSTER BIRDS OF THE MIDDLE EAST

They can pick up an elephant and carry it high up in the air,
and then they drop it, and it is completely smashed to pieces,
and then they feed on it.

~MARCO POLO, *Travels*, 1298

WHEN THE VENETIAN TRAVELER MARCO POLO was in Asia during the late 1200s, he heard a tale about the island of Madagascar, in the Indian Ocean off the coast of East Africa: "Some merchants who have been there have told me that there are griffin-birds, which appear at certain times of the year. However, they do not have the form that people here say they have, that is, half bird and half lion, but they are like eagles and are big. . . . The inhabitants of that island call this bird the rukh." Also known as the roc, the rukh was one of several gigantic birds that populated the legends, folktales, and art of Arabia, Persia, and neighboring areas.

Opposite: Carrying off an elephant, a rukh dwarfs the terrified humans below.

The Rukh

The best-known tales about the rukh come from the old Arabic stories in *The Thousand and One Nights* (or *Arabian Nights*), which were collected together between 988 and 1011. Several of these stories are about the adventurous sailor Sindbad, who had more than one encounter with the giant bird. The first time, Sindbad was stranded on an island. He was walking toward a mysterious white dome when the sky darkened, as though a heavy cloud had hidden the sun. But when he looked up at the sky, Sindbad said, "I saw that the cloud was none other than an enormous bird, of gigantic girth and inordinately wide of wing which, as it flew through the air, veiled the sun and hid it."

Sindbad continued, "I could not believe my eyes until I recalled that travellers and sailors had told me in my youth that there existed, in a far island, a bird of terrifying size called the rukh, a bird which could lift an elephant." The white dome, it turned out, was the rukh's egg, which the bird soon settled on. Once the bird fell asleep, Sindbad removed the turban from his head, unwound the long strip of cloth, and tied one end around his waist and the other to the rukh's ankle. Early the next morning "the Rukh rose off its egg and . . . with a great cry flew up into the air, dragging me with it; nor ceased to soar and to tower till I thought it had reached the limit of the firmament." Eventually the rukh landed on a hill far away from the island. Sindbad hastily untied himself and ran off to safety, but the great bird had never even noticed it was carrying him.

On a later voyage, Sindbad set sail with a group of merchants,

Hanging on to his unwound turban for dear life, Sindbad hitches a ride with a rukh.

who traded in many cities and countries until they came to an uninhabited island. There Sindbad remained in the ship while the merchants went ashore. Finding a huge white dome half buried in the sand, they started hitting it with stones. When Sindbad saw what they were doing, he immediately realized the dome was a rukh's egg, but he was too late to stop the merchants. They broke open the egg, pulled out the chick, and killed it.

Then the sky darkened as the father rukh came into view, his wings hiding the sun. "When he came and saw his egg broken, he cried a loud cry, whereupon his mate came flying up and they both began circling about the ship, crying out at us with voices louder than thunder." Sindbad urged the merchants to hurry back on board, and the crew put out to sea as quickly as possible. Everyone was relieved to see the rukhs fly away. But then "the two reappeared and flew after us and stood over us, each carrying in its claws a huge boulder which it had brought from the mountains." The male rukh dropped his rock first; it missed its target and plunged into the sea. The female rukh then dropped an even larger boulder, which crashed through the deck and smashed the rudder. The ship sank, and Sindbad survived only by hanging on to a piece of the wreckage and floating to safety.

Given such tales of the rukh's destructive powers, it was no wonder that sailors sometimes panicked at the thought of encountering the giant bird. The fourteenth-century Moroccan traveler Ibn Battuta reported what happened when his ship's crew came upon what looked like a strange mountain in the ocean just before dawn:

Later on when the sun rose we saw that the mountain had risen into the air, and that daylight was visible between it and

the sea. We were amazed at this, and I saw the crew weeping, and taking farewell of one another. So I said "What is the matter with you?" They replied "What we thought was a mountain is the Rukh, and if it sees us it will make an end of us." . . . Just then God of His mercy sent us a favourable wind, which turned us in another direction, so that we did not see it and could not learn its true shape.

Sailors continued to tell tales of the rukh for centuries to come. As late as 1579, an English writer recorded that "about the Indian sea there is a certain bird of incredible bigness, whom our countrymen call a Roche, which is able and accustomed to take up, not only a man, but also a whole ship in her beak."

PERSIA'S WINGED WONDERS

While the rukh was mainly an enemy of humans, Persian myths and legends told of a different sort of giant bird. The Senmurv had existed since the beginning of the world and helped make the earth fruitful. According to ancient scriptures, it lived in a tree "on which grow the seeds of plants of all kinds by the hundreds, thousands, and myriads." This was called the all-healing tree and the "tree without evil." Whenever the Senmurv lifted its wings and left the tree, a thousand shoots sprouted from the branches. When the Senmurv landed again, the shoots broke off and dropped their seeds. Then another great bird, named Cinamros, collected the seeds and spread them over the earth.

The Senmurv had an opposite, the monster bird Kamak. While the Senmurv created abundance, Kamak destroyed it. All he had to do was spread his wings, which covered the earth and blocked the

rainfall. Instead of watering the thirsty ground, the rain ran off Kamak's wings and back into the sea, and the land suffered from drought. Water sources dried up, crops withered, and people and animals died—either killed by thirst and starvation, or gobbled up by Kamak. Luckily there was a great hero named Keresaspa who shot arrows at Kamak day and night until the terrible creature was finally defeated.*

In the Persian poet Firdawsi's epic *Shahnameh*, completed around 1010, Keresaspa's great-grandson, Zal, owed his life to the Simorgh, as the Senmurv had come to be called by this time. When Zal was born he was a beautiful, perfect baby—except for his white hair. This seemed so unnatural that his father, Sam, thought it was an evil sign and sent little Zal away to a wild, mountainous place. Here, however, the Simorgh had her home. One day when she went out hunting for food for her chicks, she heard the abandoned baby crying.

Thanks to the Simorgh, baby Zal's story had a happy ending.

The Simorgh flew down from the clouds, stretched out her claws and clutched him, lifting him up from the hot stones on which he lay. She flew with him back to her nest. . . . When the Simorgh and her chicks looked at the little child weeping bitter tears, something wonderful to relate happened: they took pity on him, staring in astonishment at his lovely face. She sought out the most delicate morsels of the chase for the boy, touching them to his lips, and in this way many days passed and the child grew into a fine young man.

*For more of Keresaspa's adventures, see *Dragons*, another book in the CREATURES OF FANTASY series.

Meanwhile, Sam had come to regret the way he'd treated his son and set out to find him. At last he came to the mountain where the Simorgh lived. "Sam stared at the granite slopes, at the terrifying Simorgh, and at its fearsome nest, which was like a palace towering in the clouds." Seeing Sam down below, the Simorgh knew what she had to do, though she had come to love Zal. She gave him two of her feathers and told him, "If any trouble comes to you . . . throw one of my feathers into the fire, and my glory will at once appear to you." Then the Simorgh "hardened her heart for their parting and lifted him up . . . and set him down before his father."

The reunion was a joyous one, and Zal went to live with his parents in their palace. Eventually he married a young woman whom he loved very much. But when it came time for the birth of their first child, Zal's wife became deathly ill. Remembering the Simorgh's words, Zal burned one of her feathers. The great bird instantly appeared, bringing healing herbs and medical advice that saved the lives of both mother and baby. Zal became the proud father of a little boy, Rustam, who would one day be known as Persia's greatest hero. And later in life, when Rustam lay dying from battle wounds, Zal would summon the Simorgh one last time to heal his beloved son.

In a work from the early 1200s, the Persian poet Farid ud-Din Attar wrote of the Simorgh as the king of birds, who lived in isolation beyond the mountains. His home was hidden by "a hundred thousand veils of dark and light." The other birds spoke of how they owed their existence to him:

When long ago the Simorgh first appeared—
His face like sunlight when the clouds have cleared—

He cast unnumbered shadows on the earth,
On each one fixed his eyes, and each gave birth.
Thus we were born; the birds of every land
Are still his shadows—think, and understand.

Longing to see the Simorgh for themselves, the birds set out on a quest to find him. It was a grueling journey, and only thirty of the birds managed to complete it. Finally they approached the Simorgh's throne:

There in the Simorgh's radiant face they saw
Themselves, the Simorgh of the world—with awe
They gazed, and dared at last to comprehend
They were the Simorgh and the journey's end.

When the birds asked about the meaning of this, the Simorgh compared himself to a mirror, explaining, "All who come before my splendours see / Themselves, their own unique reality." After being purified by suffering on their quest, the thirty birds saw themselves when they beheld the Simorgh. In fact, *si morgh* meant "thirty birds." Farid ud-Din Attar used the play on words to help show the special kind of self-knowledge that spiritual seekers could achieve. For Attar, and for many people after him, the Simorgh was "Truth's last flawless jewel," a powerful symbol of the divine light that shines in everyone.

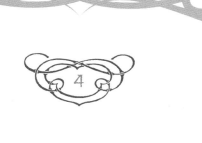

THE DEATH-DEFYING PHOENIX

It is a creature sacred to the sun, differing from all other birds.
~TACITUS, *Annals*, 1ST CENTURY

THE RUKH AND THE SIMORGH WERE NOT the only giant birds in Middle Eastern legends. Arab and Turkish lore also spoke of the *anqa* (or *angka*). It was said that God created the anqa as a perfect creature and gave it the job of eating wild animals that threatened human settlements. Eventually the huge bird—who, like the rukh, had no trouble snatching up and flying away with elephants—got greedy and devoured too many animals, so God had to banish it. The anqa was said to live for 1,700 years, after which it burned up. With its long life and its flaming death, the anqa resembled another fantastic bird: the phoenix.

Opposite:
A reborn phoenix rises from the same fire in which she died.

SACRED BIRD OF ANCIENT EGYPT

The first time the phoenix was mentioned in writing was in a poem by Hesiod, who lived in Greece during the 700s BCE. It seems the phoenix was already well known by that time, as Hesiod referred to its long life as a generally accepted fact. We can also learn a lot from the phoenix's name, which came from an ancient Greek word that could refer to a purplish-red color, to date palms, or to the land of Phoenicia (today's Israel, Palestine, and Lebanon). The name alone hints at the phoenix's color, the kind of tree it lived in, and its association with regions to the east of Greece—or generally with the east, the direction of the rising sun.

The original form of the phoenix, it seems, was the *benu* of ancient Egypt. The benu was a gigantic purple heron that was especially honored in Heliopolis, the City of the Sun. Ancient Egyptian writings have the bird saying, "I am bennu, that which is in Heliopolis. I am the keeper of the book of that which is,

An ancient Egyptian tomb painting shows the deceased worshiping the benu, an emblem of creation and rebirth.

and of that which shall be." The hieroglyph, or written symbol, of the benu meant "to shine" or "to rise." According to an Egyptian myth, before the earth took shape there was nothing but Nu, the cosmic waters. Eventually a mound emerged from Nu, and the benu landed upon it. It gave a cry that filled the world with "that which it had not known." The benu's cry was the first sound, and with it the sun rose for the first time.

Because of the benu's role at the beginning of all things, it was identified with the creator god Atum. The benu was also associated with the sun god Re (or Ra), who sailed across the sky in his solar boat each day. Re's journey began in the east with the flame-colored sunrise, and at day's end he sailed into the west, where the sky was again lit up as though on fire. From there Re descended into the underworld, the realm of the dead—but he always returned to the land of the living with the next dawn. Many Egyptians believed that Re's spirit took the form of the benu bird.

These beliefs were already thousands of years old when the Greek historian Herodotus visited Egypt in the 400s BCE. His story about the phoenix was probably his interpretation of the myth of the benu:

I have never seen the Phoenix myself save in paintings, for it is exceedingly rare and visits the land of Egypt (as I was told at Heliopolis) only at intervals of five hundred years, upon the death of the parent bird. Its plumage, judging from paintings, is partly gold and partly red, while in shape it resembles the eagle. This is the story they relate of the Phoenix: it brings its parent all the way from Arabia enclosed in a lump of myrrh and buries the body in the Temple of the Sun.

The Romans and the Phoenix

Herodotus's account was the most influential Greek telling of the phoenix legend. The most influential Roman versions were by two first-century authors, Ovid and Pliny the Elder. Toward the end of his long poem *Metamorphoses*, which retold numerous myths that involved changes from one form to another, Ovid wrote this about the phoenix:

> How many creatures walking on this earth
> Have their first being in another form?
> Yet one exists that is itself forever,
> Reborn in ageless likeness through the years. . . .
> When he has done five hundred years of living
> He winds his nest high up a swaying palm—
> And delicate dainty claws prepare his bed
> Of bark and spices, myrrh and cinnamon—
> And dies while incense lifts his soul away.

Pliny's *Natural History* gave a more straightforward account of the phoenix, which Pliny said lived in Arabia—although he was not altogether certain it was a real bird:

> The story is that it is as large as an eagle, and has a gleam of gold round its neck and all the rest of it is purple, but the tail [is] blue picked out with rose-coloured feathers. . . . [The senator Manilius] stated that nobody has ever existed that has seen one feeding, that in Arabia it is sacred to the Sun-god, that it lives 540 years, that when it is growing old it constructs a nest with sprigs of wild cinnamon and frankincense, fills it with scents and lies on it till it dies.

Pliny went on to explain that a worm emerged from the dead bird's bones. This worm quickly grew into a chick and then into an adult phoenix, which promptly carried the nest containing its parent's remains to the City of the Sun for a proper funeral.

A Roman who lived slightly later than Pliny, the historian Tacitus, noted that although most people said the phoenix lived for 500 years, others claimed its life span was 1,461 years. Tacitus added these additional details: "When the number of years is completed and death is near, the phoenix . . . builds a nest in the land of its birth and infuses into it a germ of life from which an offspring arises." As soon as the young bird was strong enough, it carried its parent to the "Altar of the Sun," where the body was burned in the holy flames. Tacitus concluded his account, "All this is full of doubt and legendary exaggeration. Still, there is no question that the bird is occasionally seen in Egypt."

Tacitus, one of ancient Rome's greatest historians, as imagined by an artist in the 1700s.

Unlike Tacitus, the early Christian leader Clement of Rome believed the entire story about the phoenix, its death, and its offspring. In a letter he wrote near the end of the first century, he emphasized that the phoenix was "the only one of its species." To Clement it was clear that the young phoenix was actually the dead bird reborn. He connected this "strange phenomenon which takes place in the East" with the miracle of Jesus's resurrection, as well as the resurrection that Jesus promised to all Christians. How could anyone doubt God's promise of eternal life, reasoned Clement, "considering that He demonstrates the greatness of his promise by means even of a bird?"

Reborn From the Ashes

The element of fire was added to the phoenix legend in the early 300s in a poem that was probably composed by a North African writer named Lactantius. He calls the phoenix "the peerless bird . . . since she lives renewed by her own death" and describes her as a priestess of the Greek sun god Phoebus Apollo. Her home is in the Grove of the Sun, where every morning she awaits the beginning of the god's daily journey and greets him with the most beautiful singing imaginable. After living a thousand years, the phoenix leaves her grove "in passion for re-birth." She flies to Phoenicia and, in the top of a palm tree, "builds herself a cradle or a sepulchre [tomb] . . . for she dies to live."

As usual, the phoenix's building materials are cinnamon, frankincense, myrrh, and other precious, fragrant substances. "Forthwith in the nest she has furnished she sets her body that awaits its change. . . . Then she commends her soul amid the varied

From a fifteenth-century German book, the phoenix in her fragrant, burning nest. She seems to be smiling as she looks forward to her rebirth.

fragrances without a fear. . . . Meanwhile her body, by birth-giving death destroyed, is aglow, the very heat producing flame and catching fire." The fire burns down to ashes, which moisture concentrates into a kind of seed. Soon a small white worm crawls out of the compacted ashes. It swiftly grows into a round egg, from which "she is remoulded in such shape as she had before, bursting her shell and springing to life a Phoenix."

The legend of the phoenix was now complete. In all the centuries since that poem was written, the phoenix has been spoken of as a one-of-a-kind, long-living bird that dies and is reborn in fire. The bestiaries of the Middle Ages followed the lead of Clement of Rome in making the phoenix a symbol of Jesus and of the resurrection. Later, the phoenix was adopted as a personal symbol by many people who had passed through difficult times and emerged victorious. For example, England's great queen Elizabeth I, who survived imprisonment and many threats to her life—and was unique in her time as a woman ruler—often used the phoenix as her emblem. Even today we speak of something that has been rebuilt or revitalized after a disaster or setback as being like a phoenix rising from the ashes.

This unique pendant, known as the Phoenix Jewel, was made between 1570 and 1580. It has a portrait of Elizabeth I on one side and on the other, the queen's phoenix emblem beneath her initials and a royal crown.

THE CHINESE PHOENIX
AND OTHERS

The phoenix sings
On that high ridge;
The dryandra grows
Where it meets the early sun.
Thick-leaved the tree,
Melodious the bird.
~"A BEND IN THE HILLSIDE," *Shijing*, AROUND 600 BCE

HE MYTHS AND LEGENDS OF CHINA AND Japan tell of fabulous birds that are often compared to the phoenix. Unlike the Western phoenix, however, these Asian birds are immortal creatures that make their home far from human lands. They rarely let themselves be seen, but when they do, it is a sign that the country is well governed and the people are living in peace and plenty. As a Chinese proverb says, "When the Dragon soars and the Phoenix dances, the people will enjoy happiness for years, bringing peace and tranquillity to all under heaven."

Opposite:
A colorful, serenely beautiful Chinese phoenix, symbol of peace, balance, and prosperity.

BIRDS OF BALANCE

The Chinese phoenix is called the *fenghuang*. It is actually a union of two birds: the male feng and the female huang. The two are often portrayed together as a symbol of true love and a happy marriage. Usually, though, artists have used the bird's combined form, an emblem of balance between male and female energies.

Many aspects of the fenghuang are symbolic. One author said that its head was like heaven, its eyes like the sun, its back like the moon, its wings like the wind, its feet like the ground, and its tail like the essence of being. According to another ancient writer, each part of the fenghuang stood for one of the five basic human qualities: the head for virtue, the wings for duty, the back for correct behavior, the breast for humanity, and the stomach for reliability. Its feathers were the five sacred colors: red, azure (a shade of blue or green), yellow, white, and black. The fenghuang's song was the five harmonious notes on which all Chinese music was based. The bird's low notes sounded like a bell, the high notes like a drum. In the morning it crowed, "I congratulate the world," and its crow at night meant, "Goodness."

It was said that the fenghuang was born in the sun. Many people believed that the bird then went to live in the paradise of the goddess known as Queen Mother of the West; paintings and other works of art sometimes showed her riding through the air on the fenghuang's back. In imperial China, the phoenix was an emblem of the empress, just as the dragon was associated with the emperor. As ruler of the 360 kinds of earthly birds, the fenghuang has been regarded as one of the four spiritual creatures that watch

The phoenix and dragon on this enameled bowl symbolize the empress and emperor of China.

over the four directions. The fenghuang's direction is the south. The other creatures are the tortoise (north); the *qilin*, or Chinese unicorn (west); and the dragon (east).

Images of the fenghuang date back to around 5000 BCE. The bird's first recorded appearance, however, was in 2647 BCE. In that year, according to legend, it flew into the garden of Huangdi, the fabled Yellow Emperor. It was Huangdi who taught the nomadic Chinese tribes to settle down, build houses, tame animals, and farm the land. The fenghuang's visit showed that the gods approved of his efforts.

The fenghuang appeared during the reigns of other great emperors, too. The bird was such an important sign of good government, peace, and prosperity that its absence became a strong sign that times were bad. The great philosopher Confucius, or K'ung-Fu-tzu (551–479 BCE), lived in an unsettled period of Chinese history and longed for the restoration of order and unity. Despairing that he would never see this during his lifetime, he exclaimed, "The fenghuang does not come; it is all over with me!"

The Ho-o and the Tengu

Like the fenghuang, the Japanese Ho-o was a combination of male (the Ho) and female (the O). It, too, was traditionally a symbol of the empress. It lived in heaven but came down from time to time to help deserving humans. Many people believed it was a messenger of the sun goddess herself.

A different sort of Japanese bird creature was the *tengu*, a spirit that lived in woodlands and mountainous regions. The king of the tengu was believed to be a giant, but most tengu were human sized or smaller. Some tengu were part human, while others would have looked like normal birds of prey if it weren't for their glowing eyes and their long red beaks curved into sneering, frowning expressions.

Suspicious of anyone who entered their territory, tengu could quickly turn hostile. They did not tolerate disrespect to themselves or to holy places, and did not hesitate to kill those who offended them. Even when tengu were simply being mischievous and playful, the outcome could be unpleasant for any humans who might be around. Tengu liked to suddenly grab people and fly off with them for a whirlwind ride through the air, usually for just a few minutes but sometimes for many hours.

Occasionally, however, someone had a positive tengu encounter. In the twelfth century an orphan boy named Yoshitsune went into the woods to practice with his sword. He was slashing away at the branches, imagining they were the enemies who had killed his father, when there was a loud thunderclap. Suddenly the king of the tengu was there before him. The giant bird frowned, annoyed that the boy had disturbed the peace of the forest. But Yoshitsune faced him so bravely that soon the tengu king's expression changed to a smile. Seeing the boy's courage and talent, the tengu offered to help him master the art of swordsmanship—an art in which the tengu were experts. Yoshitsune gratefully accepted the tengu's training and stuck with it until he became a great warrior, whose deeds are still part of Japanese history and legend today.

A nineteenth-century Japanese print shows Sojobo, the white-haired tengu king, training Yoshitsune. Tengu were believed to hatch from eggs and were originally portrayed with beaks, wings, and claws.

The Firebird

Russian folklore tells of the *zhar-ptitsa*, or "heat bird." Usually known as the Firebird, it has much in common with the phoenix and the feng-huang. It is a magical creature, rarely seen. No one knows how long the Firebird lives; it may even live forever. Its song is so enchanting that the notes take the form of pearls dropping from its beak. Its glowing feathers—red, yellow, and orange—shine in the darkness even when the bird has shed them.

The Firebird features in many old Russian stories. In one, the Firebird rescues a merchant's son from a terrible witch. In another, it saves the life of a dying prince by bringing him the Water of Life. In a fairy tale known as "Prince Ivan and the Gray Wolf" or simply "The Firebird," the bird enters a king's garden and eats the golden apples growing there. Angered, the king sends his three sons to capture the Firebird. Only Prince Ivan, the youngest, manages to succeed—but it is a long and difficult quest for him, requiring the help of a talking wolf. In 1910, composer Igor Stravinsky and choreographer Sergei Diaghilev combined the Prince Ivan story with other bits of Firebird lore and fairy-tale elements to create *The Firebird*, a ballet that has spread this fantastic Russian creature's fame throughout the world.

Above: Dancer Roberta Marquez playing the Firebird in a 2009 production of Stravinsky's ballet.

6

DANGER FROM ABOVE

We often see among the rocks the forms
of many beings that live no longer.
~ZUNI ELDERS, 1891

MORE THAN TEN THOUSAND YEARS AGO, groups of people left Asia to settle in the Americas, becoming the first humans in the western hemisphere. Many of these First Peoples found themselves sharing their new world with very large birds. As recently as eight thousand years ago, *Teratornis merriami,* a bird with a seventeen-foot wingspan, lived in regions that are now part of northern Mexico and the southern and western United States. *Teratornis* could weigh more than fifty pounds, and its beak was long and strong for snatching up prey—which might have included small humans.

The First Americans also encountered the giant condor. Today North American condors live only in California and northwestern

Opposite:
A *Teratornis merriami* fossil hangs in front of an artist's conception of what this species of giant bird looked like in life.

Mexico, but until around 1800 they lived all the way from the West Coast to New York and Florida. Modern condors, which can have a ten-foot wingspan, prey on deer as well as smaller animals, the bones of which clutter their nests. Still bigger condors lived many thousands of years ago, and scientists sometimes find their preserved nests, filled with bones from such large animals as bison and even mammoths. Early Native Americans, too, probably came across fossilized nests like these, along with fossils of huge flying reptiles from the age of the dinosaurs. With this kind of evidence around, it's little wonder that winged monsters have featured in many Native American legends.

WINGS OF TERROR

South of Syracuse, New York, Iroquois people used to point out a rock where the Great Mosquito Monster had left its tracks. This fierce creature was said to have lived in very early times, when giant bears and lions still walked the earth. According to a version of the legend told by the chief Cornplanter (1736–1836), the Great Mosquito was "an immense bird" that "would carry away children . . . or, like a bolt of lightning, dart from the sky and strike a woman or man bleeding and dying to the earth. Whole fields of corn had been destroyed in a single night by its ravages, and its coming was so swift and terrible that the Indians hardly dared stir from the shelter of their houses."

Finally a group of warriors were able to kill the terrible bird. Then people came from all the nearby villages to see the remains of their enemy: "Its body was larger than that of the largest bear they had ever seen, and the breadth of its outstretched wings was as great as the height of three men. Its talons were as long

as arrows, and its monstrous beak was lined with sharp teeth." Even in death, though, the Great Mosquito never completely left the people alone. Soon the woods became infested with "swarms of the poisonous little flies that have been the pests of all nations since that time . . . and the Indians discovered that they came from the body of the dead bird."

North and east of the Iroquois, Algonquin peoples told of the Bemola. This enormous bird had glowing red eyes and lived on Mount Katahdin in Maine. Bemola, which was sometimes called the Wind Bird, created storms, snow, and cold weather. It was respected as the guardian of the mountain but also feared because it sometimes carried people off and imprisoned them forever.

Far to the southwest, in the Sonora region of Mexico, Yaqui Indians had a similar tale. They said that long, long ago there was a giant bird that snatched up someone in its talons every evening. It took these unfortunate people to its home on Skeleton Mountain, where the slopes were littered with the bones of the bird's prey. A brave and clever orphan boy finally figured out how to kill the monstrous bird. Afterward its feathers turned into all the types of birds that exist today, while its flesh was transformed into the various kinds of clawed animals. So even though the people no longer had to fear danger from the sky, they still faced danger from "the animals of the claw."

Chief Cornplanter was a great war leader and diplomat of the Senecas, the Iroquois tribe of western New York State, during and after the American Revolution.

More than six hundred years old, this rock carving of a giant bird and its human prey can still be seen in Petrified Forest National Park in Arizona. Hopi Indians have said that it portrays a monster that terrorized their ancestors, flying down on their villages and stealing children.

In the legends of the Navajo (or Diné) of New Mexico and Arizona, there were giant birds of prey known as the Cliff Monsters. One Navajo elder described them as being "like dragons in a way"; another compared a Cliff Monster's appearance to "a great black rock which looks like a bird." Like the birds that terrorized the Yaqui and others, the Cliff Monsters had the frightening habit of carrying people away to feed to their chicks. Heroic twin warriors called the Monster Slayers killed the adult Cliff Monsters, but their chicks became the ancestors of today's eagles.

Similarly, the Cherokees of the southeastern United States had stories about the Tlanuhwa, "very large birds with markings much like the red-tail hawk. . . . Some people say the Tlanuhwa were the original parents . . . of the great hawks that live today." It was often said that Tlanuhwa carried off dogs and children. On one occasion, though, a mother Tlanuhwa snatched up a hunter. As she flew with him, she told him she did not intend to hurt him, "but only wanted him to stay for a while with her young ones to guard them until they were old enough to leave the nest." This turned out to be true, but the hunter was still afraid about what might happen to him when the chicks were grown and the mother no longer needed him. So as soon as one of the young birds was ready to fly, the hunter tied himself to its leg, and in this way he managed to escape and return to his people.

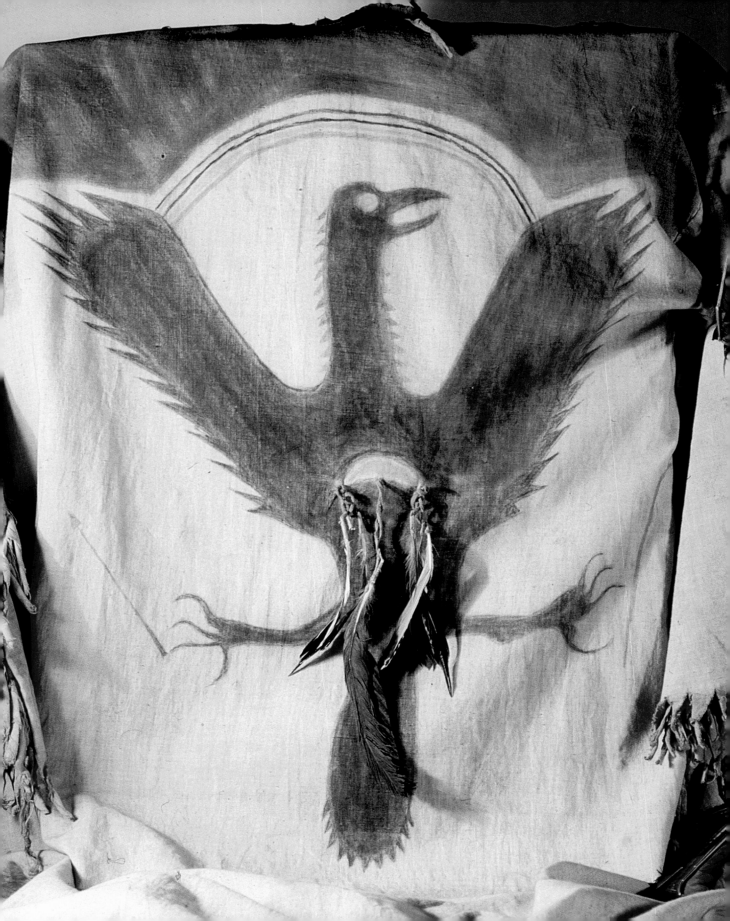

THUNDER BIRDS

Thunder often appears as a great bird,
somewhat like an eagle,
but much larger.
~George Bird Grinnell, *The Cheyenne Indians*, 1923

SOME OF THE NEW WORLD'S GIANT-BIRD legends resemble the stories we read earlier about the rukh. Indeed, there are monster birds in myths and folklore from all over the Americas and all over the world: the Xexeu bird of South America, the Hokhoku of northwestern Canada, the Ngani-Vatu of the Fiji Islands, the Pouakai of the Maori people in New Zealand, the Noga of Siberia, and more. All these creatures are gigantic, fly off with people and eat them, and usually are overcome by a great hero. Some of them also have the power to create thunder and lightning.

Native people in Alaska told this story to an anthropologist in the 1890s:

Opposite: A Thunder Bird decorates a shirt worn in Plains Indian ceremonies in the late 1800s.

Very long ago there were many giant eagles or thunder-birds living in the mountains, but they all disappeared except a single pair which made their home on the mountain top overlooking the Yukon river. . . . From their perch on this rocky wall these great birds would soar away on their broad wings, looking like a cloud in the sky, sometimes to seize a reindeer from some passing herd to bring back to their young; again they would circle out, with a noise like thunder from their shaking wings, and descend upon a fisherman in his canoe on the surface of the river, carrying man and canoe to the top of the mountain.

The story went on to tell how the Thunder Birds flew off with the wife of a young hunter, who went after them in revenge and drove them "far into the northland," so that they were never seen again.

In most legends, Thunder Birds were not so hostile to people. True, they inspired respect and caution—after all, the beating of their huge wings created thunder. Moreover, they could shoot deadly lightning bolts from their eyes, wings, beaks, or talons. In many legends, though, the great enemies of Thunder Birds were not humans, but water monsters.

MONSTER WARS

Various groups of Plains Indians knew the water monsters as Unktehi and told of great battles between them and the Thunder Birds.* It was sometimes said that the boulders scattered around the prairies had been flung at the Thunder Birds by the Unktehi.

*You can read more about the Unktehi in *Water Monsters*, another book in the CREATURES OF FANTASY series.

The great birds in turn attacked with lightning, which also left evidence behind. A Lakota Sioux holy man named Lame Deer explained that wherever there were many bones of water monsters and Thunder Birds, there were also "many *kangi tame*, bolts of lightning which have turned into black stones shaped like spear points"—actually pointed black fossils called belemnites. On the Great Plains, violent thunderstorms often washed away the soil on ridges and riverbanks, uncovering all kinds of fossils, including the bones of large prehistoric animals—some of them clearly winged.

An Assiniboine storyteller in Montana learned a tale from his grandmother in which a group of Assiniboines and Sioux actually saw a Thunder Bird and a water monster battling in a lake. The Thunder Bird grabbed the Unktehi and started to lift it into the air, which became so charged with electricity that the watching Indians felt their hair stand on end. Then the Thunder Birds let loose with bolts of lightning, which started a terrible forest fire. This was followed by a blizzard, "and still later that lake dried up and many kinds of animals perished there."

The Dakota Sioux said that the nesting ground of the Thunder Birds was a 200-mile-long plateau that straddles the border of today's Minnesota and South Dakota. Traveling artist George Catlin visited this region in 1832, and the Sioux he met there told him that whenever "the skies [were] rent with bolts of thunder," the Thunder Birds' chicks were hatching. The hatchlings, however, were frequently "destroyed by a great serpent," or water monster. This was one of the reasons for the Thunder Birds' battles with Unktehi. Another reason was that the Unktehi sometimes ate so many other creatures that nature was thrown out of balance, and only the Thunder Birds were strong enough to stop the monsters.

George Catlin made this painting of a Dakota Sioux family in 1854. The man's headdress shows that he was a mighty warrior: each eagle feather stands for an enemy he encountered face-to-face.

In Lakota Sioux beliefs, Thunder Birds were called Wakinyan, "Mysterious Flyers." There were four different types, which were easiest to tell apart by color: black, yellow, red, or blue. All were huge, with thunderous voices. They constantly fought the Unktehi, and their battlefields could be seen all along the Missouri River, wherever a bluff was collapsed. The Wakinyan also offered protection from Waziya, the north wind, which was the bringer of winter, hunger, and hardship.

Helpers and Ancestors

Thunder Birds did good in other ways, too. In a legend from the Pacific Northwest, rain, snow, sleet, and hail destroyed all the plants the people depended on for food. Ice clogged the rivers, so no one could get out to sea to go fishing, either. The starving people gathered to pray for help. "Soon there came a great noise, and flashes of lightning cut the darkness. . . . A deep, whirring sound, as of the beat of giant wings, came from the place of the setting sun. All the people turned their eyes toward the sky above the ocean as a huge, bird-shaped creature flew toward them." It was the Thunder Bird, and in its talons it gripped a gigantic whale. Gently, the Thunder Bird laid the whale on the ground in front of the amazed people, then flew off. The whale provided enough meat to sustain the people through their hard time, and "even today they never forget that visit of Thunder Bird, never forget that it ended long days of hunger and death."

In a myth recorded in British Columbia, Canada, in 1900, the Thunder Bird was a spirit being named Too-large, who lived with his wife in the Upper World. He wanted to see the Lower World, so he and his wife put on their Thunder Bird masks and came down to earth. Near a river, they saw a man struggling to build a house all by himself. When he spotted them, he commented that he wished they were people so that they could help him. When Too-large heard this, he felt moved to assist the man and exclaimed, "Oh, brother, we are people!" The story continues,

This mask made around 1900 by the Kwakiutl people of British Columbia portrays one of the supernatural birds that hunted people and took them to a being known as Man-Eater at the North End of the World.

Then Too-large and his wife took off their Thunderbird masks and ceased being birds forever. The man who had been Thunderbird said, "My name is Too-large in the Upper World, but now my name is Head-winter-dancer in this Lower World, and the name of my wife here is Winter-dance-woman." So, Head-winter-dancer and Winter-dance-woman built a house on a hill and from them came a large tribe and much greatness.

Other Native American peoples also counted Thunder Birds among their ancestors. Some Algonquin groups, for example, referred to them as "our grandfathers." Many clans, or large extended family groups, among various Northwest Coast Indians looked to the Thunder Bird as their ancestral symbol and protector. Thunder Birds are also the namesakes of a number of places in North America, such as Thunder Lake, Wisconsin; Thunder Bay, Michigan; and Thunder Bay, Ontario—all said to be traditional nesting places of the great birds.

Among the Iroquois of New York State, thunder was not a bird but a spirit named He-no or Hino. He had, however, a wise and powerful helper named Oshadagea, often called the Dew Eagle: "a great bird, whose lodge is far behind the west sky, and who carries a lake of dew in the hollow of its back." When the Fire Spirit caused droughts or forest fires, Oshadagea's messengers brought him the Earth's plea for help.

Then [Oshadagea] hears; and pluming for flight, pushes the skies far apart, obscuring the Sun with his vast spreading wings as they dip to the east and the west fanning gentle breezes, and mist veils the skies as through his fluttering wings he sifts down from his lake the dews to refresh the famishing Earth. Then all nature revives, the Fire Spirit flees; the parching Earth bares her broad breast to the falling dews; her glad rivers and lakes rejoice, and her harvests rise to new life.

Glossary

anthropologist A person who studies human societies, beliefs, and customs.

archaeologist A person who studies the tombs, ruins, art, everyday objects, and other remains of past societies.

epic A long poem about the adventures of one or more legendary heroes.

myth A sacred story; a story about divine or semidivine beings.

mythology A body or collection of myths, such as the myths of a particular people.

nomadic Refers to a society based on herding animals and moving with them from one pasture to another throughout the year.

scriptures Religious writings; holy books.

To Learn More about Griffins and Phoenixes

Books

Allen, Judy. *Fantasy Encyclopedia*. Boston: Kingfisher, 2005.

Baynes, Pauline. *Questionable Creatures: A Bestiary*. Grand Rapids, MI: William B. Eerdmans Publishing Company, 2006.

Curlee, Lynn. *Mythological Creatures: A Classical Bestiary*. New York: Atheneum Books for Young Readers, 2008.

Knudsen, Shannon. *Fantastical Creatures and Magical Beasts*. Minneapolis: Lerner, 2010.

Nigg, Joseph. *The Book of Dragons and Other Mythical Beasts*. Hauppauge, NY: Barron's, 2002.

Websites

American Museum of Natural History. *Mythic Creatures*. www.amnh.org/exhibitions/past-exhibitions/mythic-creatures

Spaid, James. *The Gryphon Pages*. www.gryphonpages.com

Selected Bibliography

Allan, Tony. *The Mythic Bestiary: The Illustrated Guide to the World's Most Fantastical Creatures*. London: Duncan Baird, 2008.

Bonfante-Warren, Alexandra. *Mythical Beasts: Traditions and Tales of Favorite Fabled Creatures*. New York: MetroBooks, 2000.

Cherry, John, ed. *Mythical Beasts*. San Francisco: Pomegranate Artbooks, 1995.

Gould, Charles. *Dragons, Unicorns, and Sea Serpents: A Classic Study of the Evidence for Their Existence*. 1886. Reprint. Mineola, NY: Dover, 2002.

Mayor, Adrienne. *The First Fossil Hunters: Paleontology in Greek and Roman Times*. Princeton, NJ: Princeton University Press, 2000.

———. *Fossil Legends of the First Americans*. Princeton, NJ: Princeton University Press, 2005.

Mercatante, Anthony S. *Zoo of the Gods: The World of Animals in Myth and Legend*. Berkeley, CA: Seastone, 1999.

Nigg, Joseph. *The Book of Dragons and Other Mythical Beasts*. Hauppauge, NY: Barron's, 2002.

———. *The Book of Fabulous Beasts: A Treasury of Writings from Ancient Times to the Present*. New York: Oxford University Press, 1999.

———. *The Book of Gryphons*. Cambridge, MA: Applewood Books, 1982.

———. *Wonder Beasts: Tales and Lore of the Phoenix, the Griffin, the Unicorn, and the Dragon*. Englewood, CO: Libraries Unlimited, 1995.

Rose, Carol. *Giants, Monsters, and Dragons: An Encyclopedia of Folklore, Legend, and Myth*. New York: W. W. Norton, 2000.

Rosen, Brenda. *The Mythical Creatures Bible: The Definitive Guide to Legendary Beings*. New York: Sterling, 2008.

South, Malcolm, ed. *Mythical and Fabulous Creatures: A Sourcebook and Research Guide*. New York: Peter Bedrick Books, 1988.

Notes on Quotations

Chapter 1

p. 9 "I hear that the griffin": Mayor, *The First Fossil Hunters*, p. 33.

p. 10 "If you don't know": Nigg, *The Book of Gryphons*, p. 25.

p. 10 "with the beak": South, *Mythical and Fabulous Creatures*, p. 92.

p. 11 "guarding in one case": Nigg, *The Book of Gryphons*, p. 43.

p. 12 "I cannot say for sure": Mayor, *The First Fossil Hunters*, p. 30.

p. 12 "Beware the sharp-beaked": Cherry, *Mythical Beasts*, p. 76.

p. 13 "Gold also is a product": Nigg, *The Book of Fabulous Beasts*, p. 44.

Chapter 2

p. 15 "The griffon is bigger": Nigg, *Wonder Beasts*, p. 52.

p. 15 "because the Griffons": Nigg, *The Book of Gryphons*, p. 50.

p. 15 "These people wage": Ibid., p. 49.

p. 16 "cruel beyond all the bounds": Cherry, *Mythical Beasts*, p. 78.

p. 16 "It is fearsome": Nigg, *The Book of Gryphons*, p. 63.

p. 16 "the cruel criminality": Cherry, *Mythical Beasts*, p. 92.

p. 16–17 "Griffins dig up gold": Ibid., p. 90.

p. 17 "the devils who" and "defend the grace": Ibid., p. 92.

p. 18 "an Emblem of valour": Nigg, *Wonder Beasts*, p. 46.

p. 18 "Griffins must be mating": Allan, *The Mythic Bestiary*, p. 44.

p. 18 "But yet the beast": Nigg, *The Book of Fabulous Beasts*, p. 233 (spelling modernized).

p. 20 "came to the immortals": Hesiod, *Theogony* 280, online at
    www.theoi.com/Ther/HipposPegasos.html

p. 21 "When he came down": Nigg, *The Book of Gryphons*, p. 57.

p. 21 "A flying creature": Nigg, *The Book of Fabulous Beasts*, p. 172.

Chapter 3

p. 23 "They can pick up": Cherry, *Mythical Beasts*, p. 96.

p. 23 "Some merchants who": Ibid., pp. 95–96.

p. 24 "I saw that the cloud": Nigg, *The Book of Fabulous Beasts*, p. 178.

p. 24 "I could not believe": Cherry, *Mythical Beasts*, p. 85.

p. 24 "the Rukh rose": Nigg, *The Book of Fabulous Beasts*, p. 178.

p. 25 "When he came" and "the two reappeared": "The Fifth Voyage of Sindbad
    the Seaman" in *The Arabian Nights*, translated by Sir Richard Burton, online at
    www.library.cornell.edu/colldev/mideast/arabnit.htm#IFTH

p. 25–26 "Later on when the sun": Nigg, *The Book of Fabulous Beasts*, p. 194.

p. 26 "about the Indian sea": Nigg, *The Book of Gryphons*, p. 31.

p. 26 "on which grow": Ilya Gershevitch, ed., *The Cambridge History of Iran*, vol. 2
    (Cambridge: Cambridge University Press, 1985), p. 644.

p. 26 "tree without evil": Hanns-Peter Schmidt, "Simorg," *Encyclopaedia Iranica*,
    www.iranica.com/articles/simorg

p. 27 "The Simorgh flew down": Firdawsi, *Shahnameh: The Persian Book of Kings*,
    translated by Dick Davis (New York: Viking Penguin, 2006), p. 64.

p. 28 "He stared": Ibid., p. 65.

p. 28 "If any trouble" and "hardened her heart": Ibid., p. 66.

p. 28 "a hundred thousand": Farid ud-Din Attar, *The Conference of the Birds*, translated
    by Afkham Darbandi and Dick Davis (London: Penguin Books, 1984), p. 33.

p. 28–29 "When long ago the Simorgh": Ibid., p. 52.

p. 29 "There in the Simorgh's radiant" and "All who come before": Ibid., p. 219.

p. 29 "Truth's last flawless jewel": Ibid., p. 220.

Chapter 4

p. 31 "It is a creature": Nigg, *Wonder Beasts*, p. 12.

p. 32–33 "I am bennu": Ibid., pp. 3–4.

p. 33 "to shine," "to rise": Nigg, *The Book of Dragons and Other Mythical Beasts*, p. 78.

p. 33 "that which it had not known": Barbara Watterson, *Gods of Ancient Egypt* (Godalming, Surrey: Bramley Books, 1999), p. 25.

p. 33 "I have never seen": Mercatante, *Zoo of the Gods*, p. 173.

p. 34 "How many creatures": Nigg, *Wonder Beasts*, p. 9.

p. 34 "The story is": Nigg, *The Book of Fabulous Beasts*, pp. 63–64.

p. 35 "When the number": Nigg, *Wonder Beasts*, p. 12.

p. 35 "Altar of the Sun" and "All this is full": Ibid., p. 13.

p. 35 "the only one" and "strange phenomenon": Nigg, *The Book of Fabulous Beasts*, p. 106.

p. 35 "considering that He": Ibid., pp. 106–107.

p. 36 "the peerless bird": Ibid., p. 85.

p. 36 "in passion for re-birth" and "builds herself a cradle": Ibid., p. 86.

p. 36–37 "Forthwith in the nest": Ibid., pp. 86–87.

p. 37 "she is remoulded": Ibid., p. 87.

Chapter 5

p. 39 "The phoenix sings": *The Book of Songs (Shijing): The Ancient Chinese Classic of Poetry*, translated by Arthur Waley (New York: Grove Press, 1996), p. 256.

p. 39 "When the Dragon soars": Rosen, *The Mythical Creatures Bible*, p. 151.

p. 40 "I congratulate" and "Goodness": Gould, *Dragons, Unicorns, and Sea Serpents*, p. 370.

p. 41 "The fenghuang does not come": Allan, *The Mythic Bestiary*, p. 36.

p. 43 "heat bird": Rosen, *The Mythical Creatures Bible*, p. 152.

Chapter 6

p. 45 "We often see": Mayor, *Fossil Legends of the First Americans*, p. 106.

p. 46 "an immense bird" and "would carry away": Canfield, William W., *The Legends of the Iroquois Told by "The Cornplanter"* (New York: A. Wessells Company, 1902), p. 59.

p. 47 "Its body was larger" and "swarms of the poisonous": Ibid., p. 61.

p. 47 "the animals of the claw": Mayor, *Fossil Legends of the First Americans*, p. 102.

p. 48 "like dragons in a way" and "a great black rock": Ibid., p. 125.

p. 48 "very large birds": David Michael Wolfe, "Legend of the Tlanuhwa and the Uhktena," www.powersource.com/cocinc/articles/tlanuhwa.htm

p. 49 "but only wanted": James Mooney, *James Mooney's History, Myths, and Sacred Formulas of the Cherokees* (Asheville, NC: Historical Images, 1992), p. 316.

Chapter 7

p. 51 "Thunder often appears": Mayor, *Fossil Legends of the First Americans*, p. 209.

p. 52 "Very long ago": Edward William Nelson, "The Eskimo about Bering Strait," *Eighteenth Annual Report of the Bureau of American Ethnology, 1896–97, Part 1* (Washington, D.C.: Government Printing Office, 1899), p. 486.

p. 52 "far into the northland": Ibid., p. 487.

p. 53 "many *kangi tame*": Mayor, *Fossil Legends of the First Americans*, p. 231.

p. 53 "and still later that lake": Ibid., p. 289.

p. 53 "the skies [were] rent" and "destroyed by": Ibid., p. 232.

p. 54–55 "Soon there came": Ella E. Clark, *Indian Legends of the Pacific Northwest* (Berkeley: University of California Press, 1953), p. 162.

p. 55 "even today they never forget": Ibid., p. 162.

p. 55 "Oh, brother" and "Then Too-large": U'Mista Cultural Society, "The Tribes," www.umista.org/kwakwakawakw/tribes.php

p. 56 "our grandfathers": Allan, *The Mythic Bestiary*, p. 16.

p. 56 "a great bird": Harriet M. Converse (Ya-ie-wa-noh) and Arthur Caswell Parker (Ga-wa-so-wa-neh), *Myths and Legends of the New York State Iroquois* (New York State Museum Bulletin 125) (Albany: University of the State of New York, 1908), p. 46.

p. 56 "Then [Oshadagea] hears": Ibid., p. 47.

INDEX

Bold page numbers indicate illustrations.

About the Author

KATHRYN HINDS grew up near Rochester, New York. She studied music and writing at Barnard College, and went on to do graduate work in comparative literature and medieval studies at the City University of New York. She has written more than forty books for young people, including *Everyday Life in the Roman Empire, Everyday Life in the Renaissance, Everyday Life in Medieval Europe,* and the books in the series BARBARIANS, LIFE IN THE MEDIEVAL MUSLIM WORLD, LIFE IN ELIZABETHAN ENGLAND, and LIFE IN ANCIENT EGYPT. Kathryn lives in the north Georgia mountains with her husband, their son, and two cats. When she is not reading or writing, she enjoys dancing, gardening, knitting, and taking walks in the woods. Visit Kathryn online at www.kathrynhinds.com